Miss Olivia Series
Lessons to Start Your Child On The Right Path of Speaking English Correctly
Olivia Korringa

Lessons to Start your Child

On The Right Path of

Speaking English Correctly

Series One

Copyright © 2009 by Olivia Korringa. 52295-KORR
Library of Congress Control Number: 2009910464
ISBN: Softcover 978-1-4415-8751-0
Hardcover 978-1-4415-8752-7

illustrations by Olivia Korringa

This book was printed in the United States of America.

To order additional copies of this book, contact:
Xlibris Corporation
1-888-795-4274
www.Xlibris.com
Orders@Xlibris.com

This Book is dedicated to

Isa

My wonderful mother who taught

Me to read before entering school.

And to

Emani

A beautiful sweet student

Who was the first to name me,

Miss Olivia

Contents

Introduction

Having had two great teachers in my life, my mother Isa and my father Knox, I in turn, had a desire to teach in the warm and caring manner that they both have.

My mother taught me to read and write through the basic phonics method of learning the sounds of the letters and by knowing the sounds, reading and spelling followed very easily.

Having learned this before entering school, made learning all other subjects that much easier. She also made sure that the English language in our home was spoken correctly.

I taught in a private school and home schooled for eleven years in New York and New Jersey.

My father Knox is a world known artist, teacher of Fine Art and is a true Art Historian.

Education is a welcome and continuing activity in our family and I am happy to be of assistance to mothers, teachers, ESL students , and children of all ages.

Look for my future series that not only cover more on the correct usage of the English language, but other topics as well.

CHAPTER 1

Lay and Lie Lesson

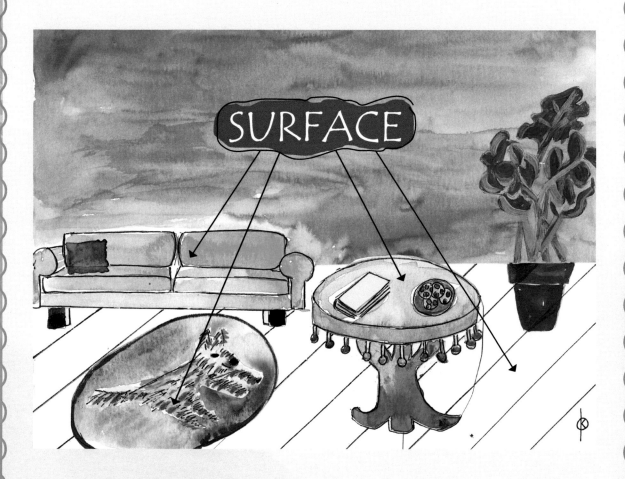

SURFACE

To learn how to use the words **lay** and **lie**, we need to learn another word first, and that word is surface.

A surface is a solid flat area, like a table, or a bed or a floor.

With your feet, feel the surface of the floor.

With your hands, feel the surface of your table.

What surface do you use to sleep on?

What surface do you put your plate on so that you can eat?

Do you have a dog or cat? What surface does it sleep on?

Point to two other surfaces in the room you are in.

Very Good!

Now we can learn the word **lie**.

Lie means to stretch out on a surface.

The way to say that you are going to stretch out on a surface is, "I am going to **lie** down".

Some people say, "I am going to lay down". This is not correct. The word lay is the way to say that you did, **lie down**.

There is another way that the word lay is used, but we will learn about this later.

If you want someone to stretch out on a surface, you say "**Lie down**". The nice way to say that is

"Please **lie down**".

To make this clear and to have fun with this word, get some paper, something to draw with, and some scissors.

Draw a boy or a girl and a dog. Cut them out. They should be big enough to play with.

Next, draw a floor with a rug. Then draw a couch big enough for your boy or girl that you made.

We can call the dog Rex. Tell Rex to **lie down**.

Take Rex and help him **lie down** on the rug.

Say, "Good Boy!" Do this a few more times until it is easy.

Now take your boy or girl and give him or her, a name.

Let's pretend that the girl's name is Jane. Have Jane say, "I am going to lie on the couch". Have her **lie** on the couch.

Have Jane say, "I am going to **lie** on the rug". Have her **lie** on the rug. You can make her **lie** on many things, but have her say where she is going to **lie**.

Great!

Here is the way that you can say that you <u>did</u> **lie down**.

That word is **Lay**. I **lay** down on the couch. Rex **lay** on the rug all day.

The other way that **lay** is used, is when you want someone to place something down on a surface. "Please **lay** the dishes on the table". Please **lay** the blanket on the bed".

Lay, is also used when you want to say that you are going to place something down on a surface. "I will **lay** the baby in the crib". "I will **lay** the book on the table". "Jane will **lay** the cat on the floor".

When you have placed something like a book down on a surface such as a table, you would say, I **laid** the book on the table. To say that you did **lie** on the bed this morning, you'd say, I **lay** on the bed this morning.

To say that Rex placed his bone on the rug. You would say, Rex **laid** his bone on the rug.

The word **lying** is used to say that you did **lie** down or that you are doing that.

I am **lying** on the bed. He is **lying** on the couch. I was **lying** on the beach.

Read this story or have a grown up read it to you.

Mary was very sleepy and decided to **lie** down to take a nap. She quickly fell asleep and dreamed that she was **lying** in the forest and all around her **lay** pine cones from the big pine trees.

The sun's rays shone down on the pine cones making the air warm and sweet.

A cute bunny came hopping close to her and **laid** his paw on her hand. She was not afraid and loved the little bunny.

Mary woke up from her dream and was smiling. Mary got up from the bed where she had been **lying** and smoothed out the covers so that it was just as it was before she **lay** on it for her nap.

Read and fill in with your own words:

I **lay** on the _____this morning.

Tommy **lays** the _____on the table.

I **laid** all the plates on the _____.

I want my kitten to **lie** on my _____.

Mary **lay** down on the couch to watch _____.

Let's **lie** down and read _____ together.

Miss Olivia says, "Very Good"

CHAPTER 2

The Any Lesson

We are going to learn about a word that we use every day.
It is the word **Any**.
Any means, even one thing or a little of something.
Here are some ways that we use the word **any**:
Do you have **any** cookies?
Do you have **any** candy?
Do we have **any** toys to play with?

You also need to use the word **any** to show what you don't have.
Like this:
I don't have **any** cookies.
I don't have **any** candy.
We don't have **any** toys to play with.
You need to show what you don't have, so that is what the word **any** does too. It shows what you don't have.

To really understand this better, get some paper, something to draw with, and some scissors. On one sheet of paper, draw a big plate. Cut out the plate.

On another sheet of paper, draw 6 cookies and cut them out.

Now, take the cookies and put them all on the plate.

Do you have **any** cookies? The answer is yes.

Now pretend to eat all the cookies. Look at the plate.

Do you have **any** cookies? The answer is no.

There is a word that we use which is made up of two words to make it shorter to say.

The word is, **don't**. The long way to say it is, **do not**.

Look at the plate and say,

I **don't** have **any** cookies. You can play with the cookies by putting them on the plate and ask, do I have **any** cookies? Then take them away and say, I don't have **any** cookies. You can play this game with another person.

The next part of this lesson is about how some people say that they don't have something, but it is not the right way to say it.

They say, "I don't got no cookies." When Miss Olivia hears this, it feels like squeaking chalk on a blackboard.

The first thing to notice about this sentence is it is really saying that you have cookies.

Do you see **any** cookies? Yes, I see five cookies.

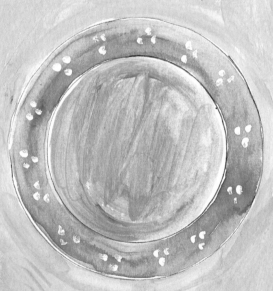

Do you see **any** cookies? No. I don't see **any** cookies.

Here are the **wrong** ways to say that you don't have **any** cookies:

I don't have no cookies.

I don't got no cookies.

I got no cookies. (When you are talking about having)

This last one would be right if you are talking about taking or getting cookies, but not about having them.

Remember the right way?

I don't have **any** cookies.

Doesn't, is a short way to say **Does Not**.

You can say she **doesn't** have **any** cookies.

He **doesn't** have **any** cookies.

Read this story or have a grown up read it to you.

Count how many times you read or hear the word **any**.

Sandra and Billy were good friends. They lived near the beach. One sunny morning, they went for a walk near the water to look for sea shells. Sandra said, "Do you see **any** orange sea shells?" Billy looked and said "yes, I see some over there!". They collected many pretty shells. Some were yellow, some were white and some were orange. "We don't need to get **any** more shells", Sandra said. They decided to sit down on the sand and enjoy the beautiful waves and blue sky. There weren't **any** clouds in the sky. Soon they were hungry. Sandra had some cheese sandwiches in her bag. Sandra and Billy sat near the pretty shells to eat. Soon there were seagulls landing near them. They wanted some food. Billy threw some bread into the air and a gull snatched it. Sandra and Billy laughed. It was fun to see. Sandra asked, do you have any more bread? Billy said, "No, I don't have **any** more bread, do you?" Sandra said, "Yes". Sandra shared her bread with Billy and they both threw the bread into the air, laughing as the gulls ate it all. There wasn't **any** bread left.

Billy and Sandra gathered the shells and put them in Sandra's bag. They walked home feeling happy.

CHAPTER 3

Got and Have Lesson

The word **got** means that you were given something, or that you took something.

I **got** a large kite for my birthday.
I **got** the ball from under the bed.
Mary **got** a new dress yesterday.
John **got** the letter he was waiting for.
I **got** the mail, it is on the table.

Get is the word used to say that you will be given something or that you want someone to take something or that you will take something.

I will **get** a new bike for my birthday.
Will you **get** the milk from the store?
I am going to **get** the mail.

I HAVE

Have means that you own something or that something is with you.

I **have** two new toys.
I **have** pizza for lunch.
I **have** the ball that you were looking for.

The lesson being taught is that some people use the word **got**, when they should use the word **have**.

Here is the <u>wrong</u> way to use the word "**got**", if you are trying to say that you own something.

I got a bike.
I got a TV
I got five shirts.

Here is the <u>right</u> way to say that you own something.

I **have** a bike.
I **have** a TV.
I **have** five shirts.

If you want to say that you were given those things or that you took or paid money for those things.
Then you <u>would</u> use the word "**got**".

I **got** a bike for my birthday.
I **got** a TV from the store.
I **got** five shirts from the cleaners.
I **got** the umbrella from the closet.

There is a word that will help us that is really made up of two words.

One of the words is "**I**", and that is used to talk about you.
The other word is "**Have**", which we learned and it means that you own something.

The word that is made up of these two words is a short way of saying "**I have**".

It is "**I've**".

It is used like this:
I've got some new pens.
I've got a new friend.
I've got a game that we can play together.

To say "I got a new friend", is leaving out the second word "**have**". You could say "I have got a new friend", but people like to have a short way to say things sometimes and the short way to say "**I have**", is "**I've**".

"**I've** got two red pens".
"**I've** got many friends".
"**I've** got a dog and a cat".

This is to show what you own, so the word is "**have**". Whether you say it the long way, "**I have**", or the short way, "**I've**".

And the way to say that someone gave you something or that you took something, is "**Got**".

Now that we have learned those words, we can use them.

Get some paper and draw a girl big enough to cut out with scissors. Now draw a boy, a dog, two phones and a doggy bone. Cut them out too.

We'll call the girl Sally and the boy Peter. The dog can be called Rex or whatever name you choose.

Let us pretend that it is a day after Peter's birthday.

You can help Sally and Peter talk on the phone.

Have Sally call Peter on the phone.

Hi Peter! This is Sally. Hi Sally! You can be both voices.

What presents did you **get** for your birthday, Peter?

I **got** some new games. I **got** two shirts from my Aunt. I also **got** a skate board!

Have Sally say, "That is really nice!"

Did you **get** anything else?

Have Peter say, "No, but my Uncle gave me some money, and I am going to **get** a new basket ball, because the one that I have has a hole in it.

Have Sally say, "That is nice! Do you want to go to the ice cream shop with my mother and me? Have Peter say, "I **have** a better idea, why don't you come here with your mother?" I **have** a lot of ice cream cake left from my party." **I've got** the new games that we can play together". Have Sally say,

"Okay, we will be over very soon. Have them say "Bye", to each other.

Peter told his mother that he asked Sally and her mother to come over to have cake and for Sally to play some games with him.

Peter's mother was happy and began to get things ready for their visit.

While Peter is waiting for Sally and her mother to get to his house, have Peter play outside with his dog Rex. Have Peter show the bone to Rex.

Have Peter say, "Rex! **Get** the bone! And help Peter throw the bone. Have Rex run after it and **get** the bone. Have Rex run back to Peter. Have Peter say, "Good Boy! You **got** the bone! Let me **have** the bone." Make Rex drop the bone. Make Peter say, "Good Rex!" Make Peter throw the bone again and make him say, Rex, **get** the bone! Do this until it is easy and you know how to use **got** and **get**.

Sally and her mother came to Peter's house and they all had a wonderful time eating ice cream cake and playing games.

Practice saying these sentences:

    I have _____(fill in with something that
you own).

    I've got _____(Fill in with something that
you own)

    I got _____(Fill in with something that
someone gave you)

    I got _____(Fill in with something that
you took)

    Miss Olivia is very proud of all the learning you have
done in this book.
    Your life will be better with your new speaking skills.
    Miss Olivia has more lessons for you.
    Look for her books in the near future.

    I love you! Miss Olivia ☺

Get Published, Inc!
Thorofare, NJ 08086
28 January, 2010
BA2010028